Sergei Prokofiev

FOUR ORCHESTRAL WORKS

Classical Symphony
Lieutenant Kije Suite
Peter and the Wolf
Alexander Nevsky Cantata

Selected and Edited by Lewis Roth

DOVER PUBLICATIONS, INC., NEW YORK

contained, in Russian only, the following information about those three works, translated here for the first time.

Concerning the *Lieutenant Kije Suite:*

"*Lieutenant Kije*, Op. 60, a suite based on the incidental music for the film, was written in 1934. At the time of Prokofiev's arrival in Moscow and Leningrad [from abroad, 1932], the idea arose of employing his talents for the composition of the music of the film *Lieutenant Kije*, based on the story by Y. N. Tynyanov, which was being produced in the Byelgoskino studio. In his essay 'What Kind of Subject Do I Look For?' Prokofiev wrote: 'There is a project for work on the musical setting of the sound film *Lieutenant Kije* (based on Y. N. Tynyanov's story of the same name). I am negotiating with the Byelgoskino film studio on this matter.'

"In his *Autobiography*, when describing his life in 1933, Prokofiev wrote: 'On my return to Moscow I began my work on the *Lieutenant Kije* film score with pleasure. Somehow I had not a single doubt concerning the musical language for this film. I traveled to Leningrad for the recording of the score. [I. O.] Dunayevsky conducted it pretty intelligently. Unfortunately the denouement of the plot was repeatedly changed, which made the film confusing and sluggish. The following year I wrote a symphonic suite, on which I spent considerably more time than I had spent on the film score, since I had to work out the form, reorchestrate, add finishing touches and even combine themes.'

"The first performance of the *Lieutenant Kije Suite* took place in Moscow on December 21, 1934, under the composer's direction. The score of the suite was published in 1935 by the house of A. Gutheil."

Concerning *Peter and the Wolf:*

"*Peter and the Wolf*, Op. 67, a symphonic tale for children, written for orchestra and narrator, was composed in 1936. In his *Autobiography*, Prokofiev wrote: 'The need for music for children made itself plainly felt, and in the spring of 1936 I began the symphonic tale for children *Peter and the Wolf*, Op. 67, to my own text. Every character in the tale had his own leitmotiv, always entrusted to the same instrument: I depicted the duck by the oboe, the grandfather by the bassoon, and so on. Before the start of the performance the instruments were shown to the children and the themes were played on them; during the performance the children heard the themes repeatedly and learned to differentiate the timbres of the instruments—herein lay the educational purpose of the piece. The text was read in short segments during pauses in the music, which was disproportionately long in comparison to the text; what was important to me was not to tell a story, but to have the children listen to the music, for which the story was merely a pretext. I wrote the music quickly, in about a week, and I spent about the same amount of time orchestrating it.'

"The first performance of the tale *Peter and the Wolf* took place in Moscow on May 2, 1936, under the composer's direction; the narrator was T. Bobrova. As the composer wrote, 'The performance was indifferent and little attention was paid to *Peter and the Wolf*.' Interesting details on the purpose and composition of the tale *Peter and the Wolf* are contained in the reminiscences of N. I. Sats, 'How the Tale *Peter and the Wolf* Was Created.' Prokofiev himself was very fond of this composition and conducted it in Boston during his last trip abroad in the winter of 1937/1938."

Concerning the *Alexander Nevsky Cantata:*

"*Alexander Nevsky*, Op. 78, a cantata for mezzo-soprano, mixed chorus and orchestra, to a text by V. A. Lugovskoy and Prokofiev, was written in 1938 and 1939. It was based on the music from the film [by Eisenstein] of the same name, produced in 1938. Concerning the composition of the film music Prokofiev wrote: 'Those who saw the film recall that the Teutonic Knights, advancing for their attack, sing Catholic psalms. Since the action took place in the thirteenth century, I was interested first of all in the kind of music sung by Catholics at that time. I borrowed a book from the library of the Moscow Conservatory that contained a collection of Catholic hymns of various centuries. What did I find? This music was so alien to us that I had to give up the idea of using it in the film. No doubt the Knights, when marching into battle, sang it in a sort of frenzy, but nonetheless it gave present-day ears the impression of being cold and passionless. As a result I was compelled to reject it and compose music for the Knights that would best express the required atmosphere for contemporary viewers.'

"The cantata was first performed in Moscow on May 17, 1939, under the composer's direction. The mezzo-soprano role was sung by V. Gagarina. The score of the cantata was first published by Muzgiz in 1941."

CLASSICAL SYMPHONY

Op. 25 (1916–1917)

Dedicated to Boris Vladimirovich Asafiev

Instrumentation

2 Flauti	2 Flutes
2 Oboi	2 Oboes
2 Clarinetti	2 Clarinets
2 Fagotti	2 Bassoons
2 Trombe	2 Trumpets
2 Corni	2 Horns
Timpani	Timpani
Violini I	Violins I
Violini II	Violins II
Viole	Violas
Violoncelli	Cellos
Contrabassi	Double Basses

Clarinets, Trumpets and Horns are notated in the score in C, i.e. as they sound. The transposition in the parts should be Clarinet in A, Trumpet in B♭, Horn in F.

I

II

III
Gavotte

III A.
Gavotte
(New expanded version)

IV
Finale

LIEUTENANT KIJE SUITE

Op. 60 (1934)

From the Incidental Music to the Film

Instrumentation

Piccolo	Piccolo
2 Flauti	2 Flutes
2 Oboi	2 Oboes
2 Clarinetti	2 Clarinets
Saxofono tenore	Tenor Saxophone
2 Fagotti	2 Bassoons
Cornetto a pistone	Cornet
2 Trombe	2 Trumpets
4 Corni	4 Horns
3 Tromboni	3 Trombones
Tuba	Tuba
Triangolo	Triangle
Sonagli	Sleigh Bells
Tamburino	Tambourine
Tamburo	Snare Drum
Piatti	Cymbals
Gran cassa	Bass Drum
Celesta	Celesta
Arpa	Harp
Piano	Piano
Violini I	Violins I
Violini II	Violins II
Viole	Violas
Violoncelli	Cellos
Contrabassi	Double Basses

In the score all the instruments are written in C, i.e. as they sound. In the parts, however, clarinets, tenor saxophone, cornet and trumpets should be in B♭, horns in F. In the score accidentals for cornet, trumpets and horns are shown in the key signature; in the parts the accidentals for these instruments should be written next to the notes.

The celesta and piano parts should be incorporated into one part, which can be played by one musician. If no celesta is available, its part may best be performed by the orchestra bells, but may also be taken by the piano; in the latter case the right hand must play an octave higher, while the left hand plays as written.

The designation *Sonagli* indicates the collar [of the *troika* horses] with its little bells. The percussion should be grouped in the following way:

1. Triangle and Bass Drum
2. Tambourine, Snare Drum and Cymbals
3. Sleigh Bells

In the tambourine part in the fourth movement, a circle over a note indicates that the instrument should be struck with the fist, while on the notes without a circle the tambourine is to be shaken. At the beginning and end of the first and fifth movements, the cornet should play its solo part offstage (*in distanza*), but should play the rest of its part in the orchestra.

If no cornet is available, it can be replaced by the first trumpet, its music being cued into the first-trumpet part. In the same manner, if there is no saxophone, its part may be played by the first bassoon, but not when the suite is performed without a singer (in other words, it should be performed either with a vocalist or with a saxophone).

This suite can be performed with or without a (baritone) singer. The vocal part will be found in movements No. 2 and No. 4; if the suite is performed without a singer, it should be played with movements No. 2A and No. 4A.

Correspondingly, there will be a No. 2 and a No. 2A, and a No. 4 and a No. 4A, in the parts as well. Those parts where the instruments play the same music in both cases, should carry the notice: "No. 2 or 2A," "No. 4 or 4A."

The conductor should take note when the fourth movement is performed with a vocalist, the accompaniment should be played a little more softly, but without the vocal part it should be more vigorous.

No.1. Kije's Birth

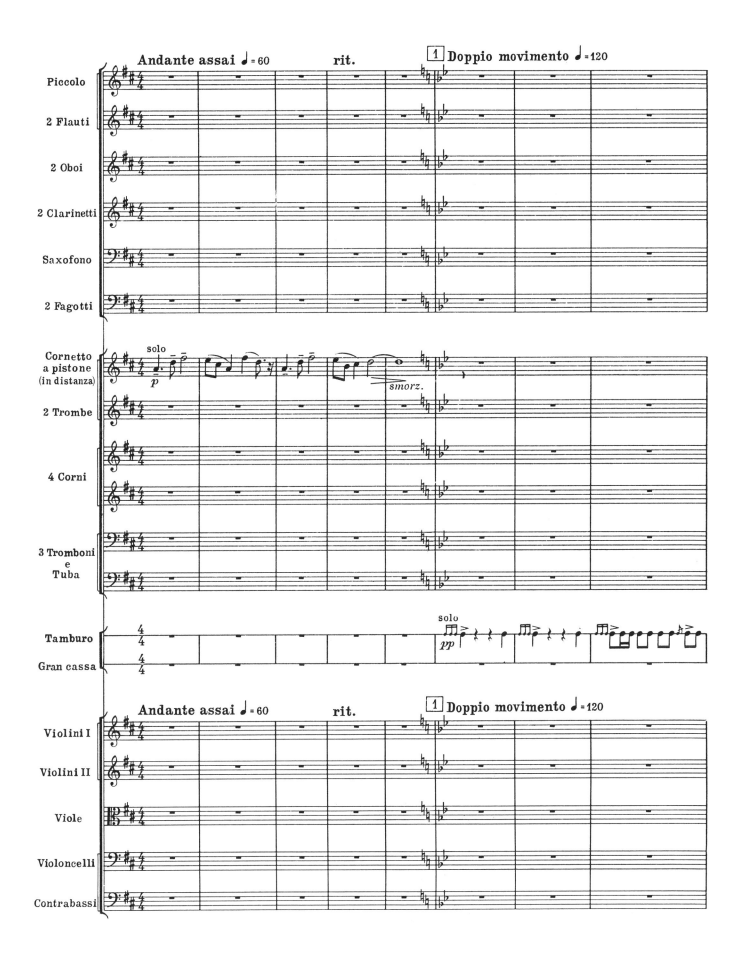

No. 2. Song

он и день и ночь. Е - го ми - лень-кой дру-жо-чек от - - ле-тел да-ле-ко прочь.

Полно, серд-це, ус-по-кой-ся, пол-но ба-боч-кой ле-тать! пол-но ба-боч-кой ле-тать.

Пол - но, серд-це, ус - по-кой-ся, пол-но, пол-но ба-бочкой летать.

Сердце бед-но-е за-би-лось и не зна-ло, как нам быть.

Сто - нет си - зый го - лу - бо - чек, сто - нет

No. 2 A. Song
(variant without text)

No. 3. Kijé's Wedding

No. 4. Troika Song

ут - ра до ут - ра. Серд - ца у жен - щин как трак - тир: про -

хо - лост и - ли кто же - нат, кто ро - бок и - ли

холост иль же - нат, кто ро - бок иль не ро - бок, и - ли ро - бок и - ли хват. Ах,

подь сю - ды, да подь сю - ды, не бойсь со мной бе - ды. Серд - ца у жен - щин

как трак - тир: про - хо - жих це - лый _ мир.   От

No. 4 A. Troika Song
(variant without text)

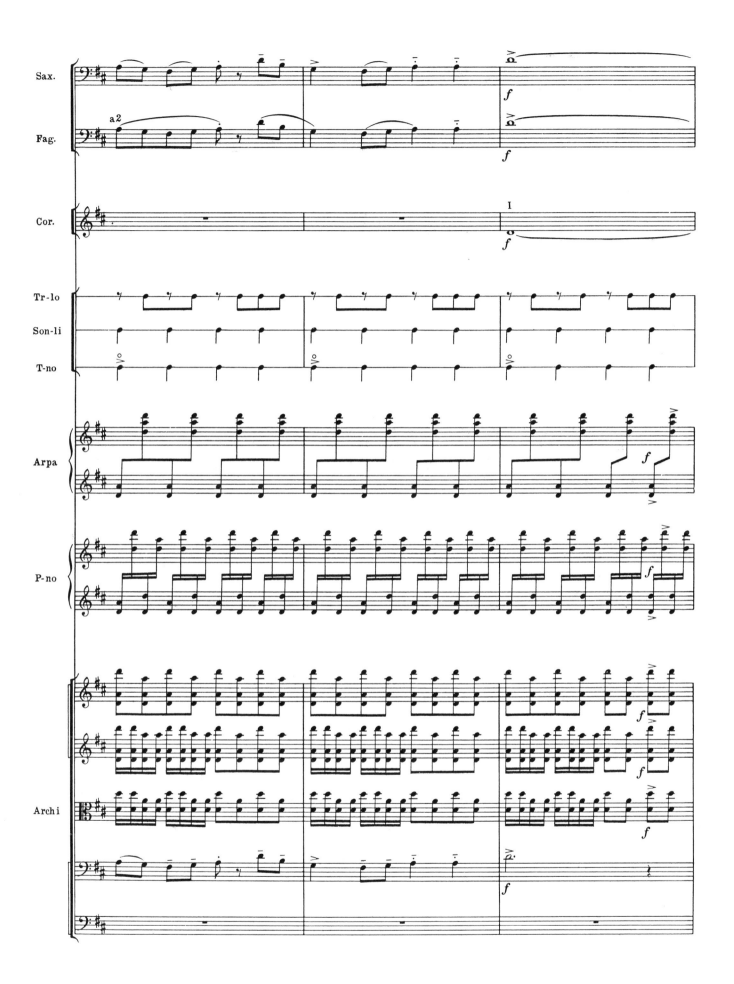

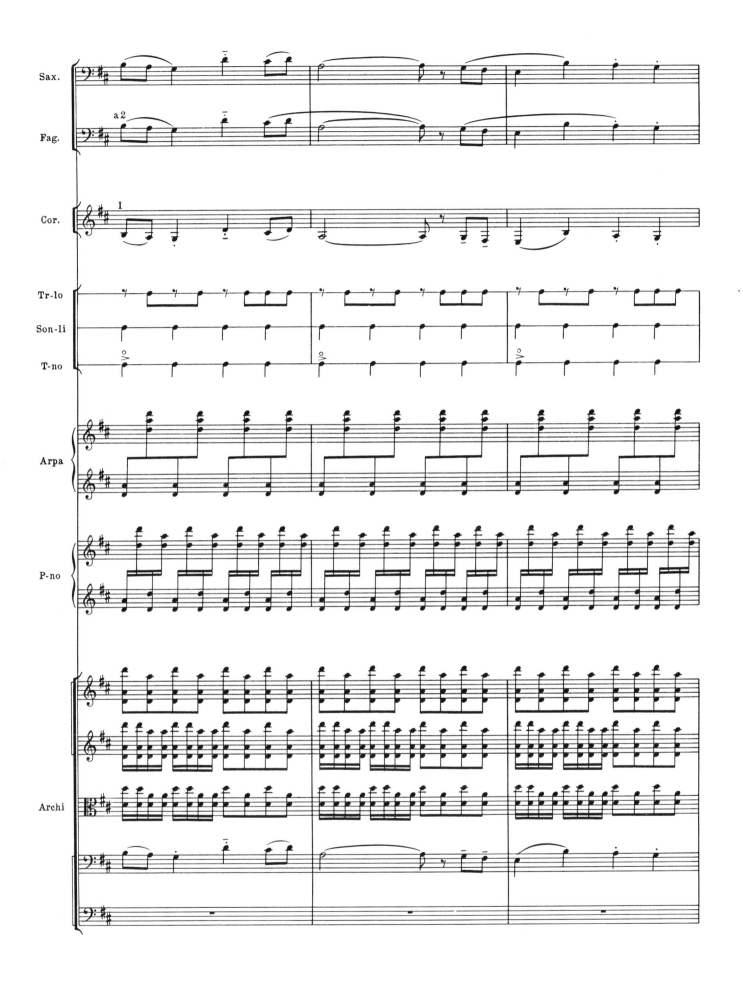

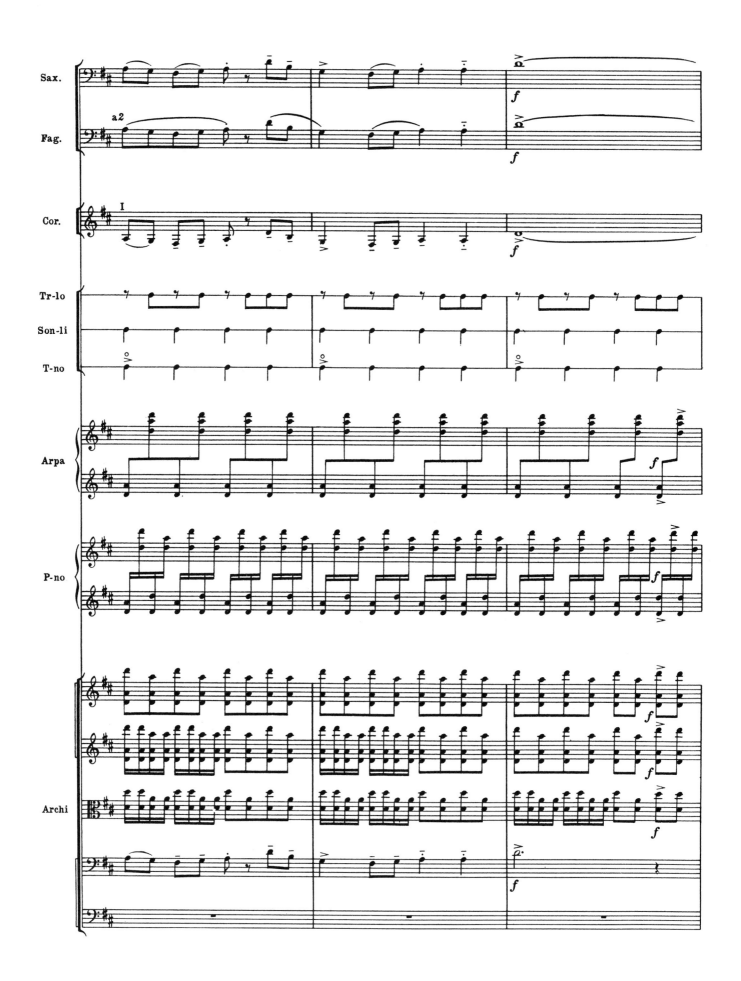

No. 5. Kije's Burial

Translations of Song Texts

No. 2: Song

The gray dove moans, he moans day and night. His beloved sweetheart has flown far away. He no longer coos, but only grieves and grieves. From one tender branch to another he flits, and awaits the arrival of his dear companion from all sides. Enough, my heart, grow calm, flutter no longer like a butterfly. Try, without fear, to gain another nook. The heart has begun to seek. Enough, my heart, grow calm, flutter no longer like a butterfly. How, then, my heart: have you decided where we shall dwell in summer? My poor heart began to throb, and did not know how we were to exist. The gray dove moans, he moans day and night. His beloved sweetheart has flown far away. The gray dove moans.

No. 4: Troika Song

The heart of woman is like an inn: it has a whole world of guests. From morn to morn, someone drives into the courtyard and someone drives out. Someone drives in, someone drives out, and so it goes from morn to morn. The heart of woman is like an inn: it has a whole world of guests. From morn to morn, someone drives into the courtyard and someone drives out. Ah, come here, yes, come here, don't be afraid that I'll do you any harm. One fellow is single, one is not, one is single, one is married. One is shy, one is not, one is shy, one is a daredevil. Ah, come here, yes, come here, don't be afraid that I'll do you any harm. One is single, one is married, one is shy, one is a daredevil. Ah, come here, yes, come here, don't be afraid that I'll do you any harm. Hey! Hey! Hey! Hey! So from morn to morn, someone drives in, someone drives out, and so from morn to morn. Ah, come here, yes, come here, don't be afraid that I'll do you any harm. One is single, one is married, one is shy, one is a daredevil. Ah, come here, yes, come here, don't be afraid that I'll do you any harm. The heart of woman is like an inn: it has a whole world of guests. From morn to morn, someone drives into the courtyard and someone drives out.

PETER AND THE WOLF

Op. 67 (1936)

Symphonic Tale for Children
For Narrator and Orchestra

Instrumentation

Flauto	Flute
Oboe	Oboe
Clarinetto	Clarinet
Fagotto	Bassoon
Tromba	Trumpet
3 Corni	3 Horns
Trombone	Trombone
Timpani	Timpani
Triangolo	Triangle
Castagnetti	Castanets
Tamburino	Tambourine
Tamburo	Snare Drum
Piatti	Cymbals
Gran cassa	Bass Drum
Violini I	Violins I
Violini II	Violins II
Viole	Violas
Violoncelli	Cellos
Contrabassi	Double Basses

Each character of this tale is depicted by its own instrument in the orchestra: the bird by a flute, the duck by an oboe, the cat by a clarinet playing staccato in a low register, the grandfather by a bassoon, the wolf by three horns playing in chords, Peter by the string section, the shooting of the hunters by the timpani and bass drum. Before the orchestra performance, it is desirable to show these instruments to the children and to play the leitmotivs on them. In this way the children, during the performance, will easily learn to distinguish the sonorities of these orchestral instruments.

In the score all the instruments are written in C, i.e. as they sound. In the parts, however, the clarinet should be in A, the trumpet in Bb, and the horns in F.

In the score, horn and timpani accidentals are shown in the key signature; in the parts the accidentals for these instruments should be written next to the notes.

The percussion should be grouped as follows:
1. Timpani, Triangle, Tambourine, Cymbals
2. Castanets, Snare Drum, Bass Drum

Andantino ♩ = 92
Рано утром пионер Петя открыл калитку
и вышел на большую зеленую лужайку.

Early one morning Peter opened the gate and
went out into the big green meadow.

На высоком дереве сидела Петина
знакомая птичка. „Все вокруг спо-
койно-“, весело зачирикала она.

On the branch of a large tree sat a little
bird, Peter's friend. "Everything is
quiet," chirped the bird gaily.

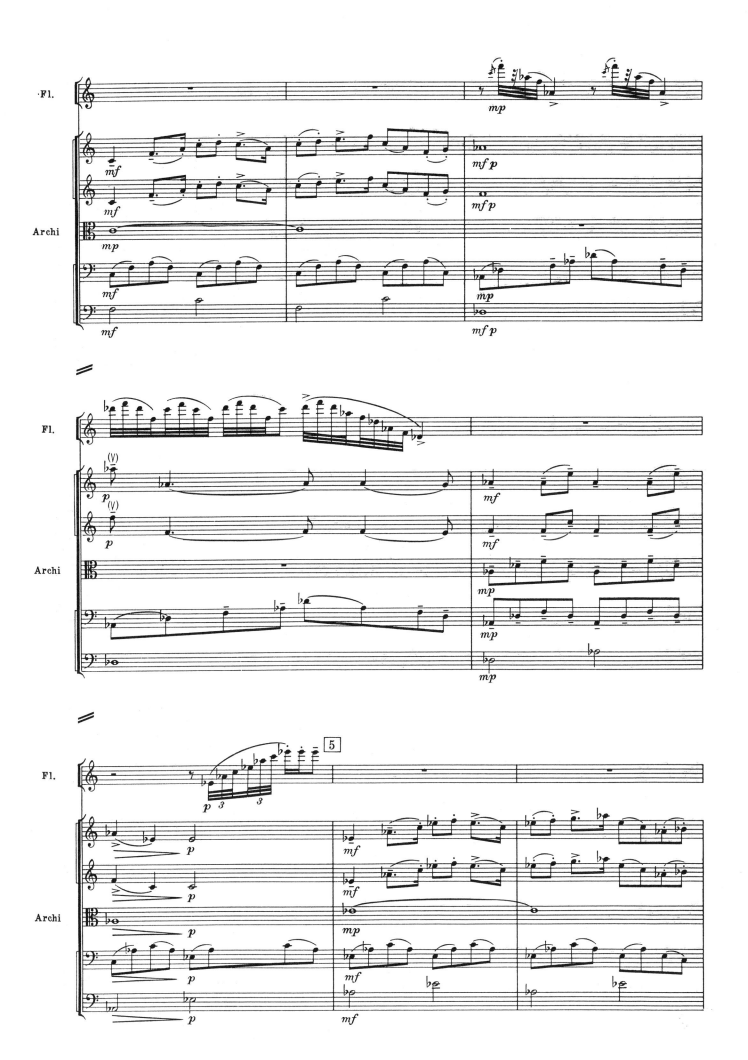

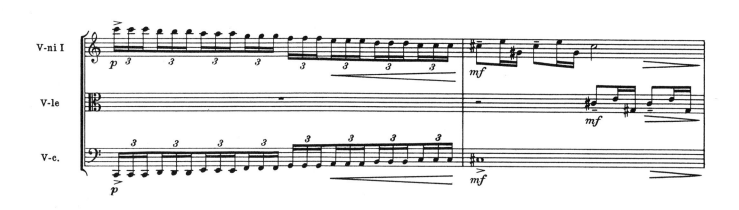

Вслед за Петей, переваливаясь с боку на бок, показалась утка. Она обрадовалась, что Петя не закрыл калитку, и решила выкупаться в глубокой луже на лужайке.

Soon a duck appeared, waddling from side to side. It was glad that Peter had not closed the gate, and it decided to take a nice swim in the deep pond in the meadow.

Увидев утку, птичка слетела на траву,
села рядом с уткой и пожала плечами:

Seeing the duck, the little bird flew down upon
the grass, settled next to the duck and shrugged
its shoulders:

„Какая же ты птица, если ты летать не умеешь!"–сказала она.
На что утка ответила: „Какая же ты птица,если ты плавать
не умеешь!" и плюхнулась в лужу.

"What kind of bird are you, if you can't fly!" it said. To which
the duck replied: "What kind of bird are you, if you can't swim!"
and dived into the pond.

accel.

Они еще долго спорили- утка, плавая по луже, птичка, прыгая по берегу.

They argued and argued—the duck swimming in the pond, the little bird hopping along the bank.

Вдруг Петя насторожился. Он заметил, что по траве крадется кошка.

Suddenly something caught Peter's attention. He noticed a cat slinking through the grass.

Кошка подумала: „Птичка занята спором?
Сейчас я ее сцапаю." И неслышно, на бар-
хатных лапках подбиралась к ней.

The cat thought: "The bird is busy arguing. I'll
just grab it." Stealthily it crept toward the bird
on velvet paws.

"Look out!" shouted Peter, and the bird
immediately flew up into the tree.

А утка из середины
своей лужи

While the duck quacked
angrily at the cat . . .

... from the middle of the pond.

Кошка ходила вокруг дерева и думала: „Стоит ли лезть так высоко? Пока влезешь, птичка всё равно улетит."

The cat walked around the tree and thought; "Is it worth climbing up so high? By the time I get there the bird will surely have flown away."

Вышел дедушка. Он сердился,
что Петя ушел за калитку.
Места опасные. Если из лесу
придет волк, что тогда?

Grandfather came out. He was
angry because Peter had gone
past the gate into the meadow. It
is a dangerous place. If a wolf
should come out of the forest, what
then?

Петя не придал никакого значения словам дедушки
и заявил, что пионеры не боятся волков.

Peter paid no attention to Grandfather's words, and declared
that boys like him are not afraid of wolves.

Но дедушка взял Петю за руку, увел
домой и крепко запер калитку.

But Grandfather took Peter by the hand,
led him home and locked the gate fast.

(senza rit.)

Ob.

Cl.

Fag.

Timp.

И действительно, не успел
Петя уйти, как из лесу пока-
зался огромный серый волк.

Archi

And indeed, no sooner had
Peter gone, than an enormous
grey wolf came out of the
forest.

19 **Andante molto** ♩ = 66

Cl.

Cor.

P-tti

V-le

V-c.

C-b.

Кошка быстро полезла на дерево.

The cat quickly climbed up the tree.

Утка закрякала и бросилась
вон из лужи.

The duck quacked and in its
excitement jumped out of the
pond.

схватил... и проглотил.

and then he caught it . . . and with one gulp
swallowed it.

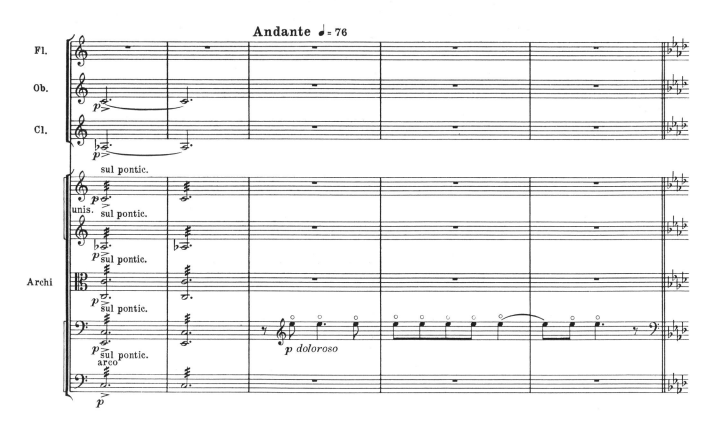

Теперь картина была такая:
кошка сидела на одной ветке,

And now, this is how things
stood: the cat was sitting on one
branch,

птичка на другой...   подальше от кошки.

the little bird on another . . .   . . . not too close to the cat.

А волк ходил вокруг дерева и смотрел
на них жадными глазами.

And the wolf walked round and round the tree
looking at them with greedy eyes.

28 Andantino, come prima ♩ = 92

Между тем пионер Петя, который остался
стоять за запертой калиткой и видел всё
происходящее, нисколько не испугался.

In the meantime, Peter, without the slightest
fear, stood behind the locked gate watching all
that was going on.

Он побежал домой, взял толстую верёвку и влез на высо-
кий каменный забор.

He ran home, got a strong rope and climbed up the high stone wall.

Одна из веток дерева, вокруг которого ходил волк, простиралась до этого забора.

One of the branches of the tree around which the wolf was walking stretched out over the wall.

29

И, ухватившись за нее,

Grabbing hold of the branch,

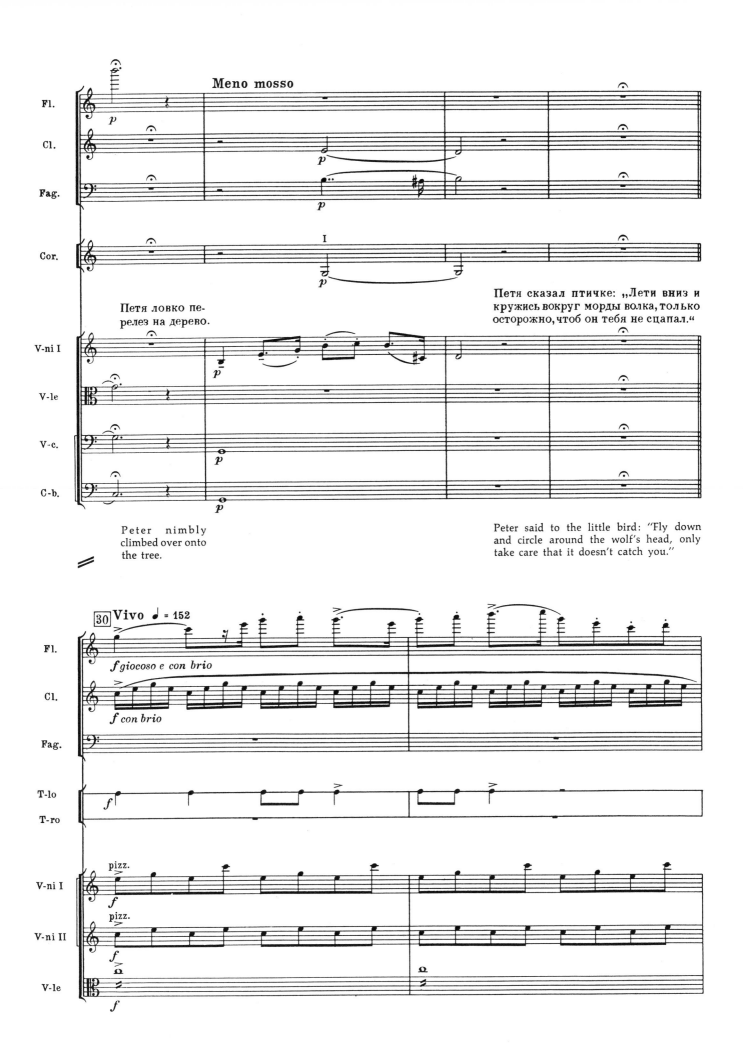

Петя ловко пе-
релез на дерево.

Петя сказал птичке: „Лети вниз и
кружись вокруг морды волка, только
осторожно, чтоб он тебя не сцапал."

Peter nimbly
climbed over onto
the tree.

Peter said to the little bird: "Fly down
and circle around the wolf's head, only
take care that it doesn't catch you."

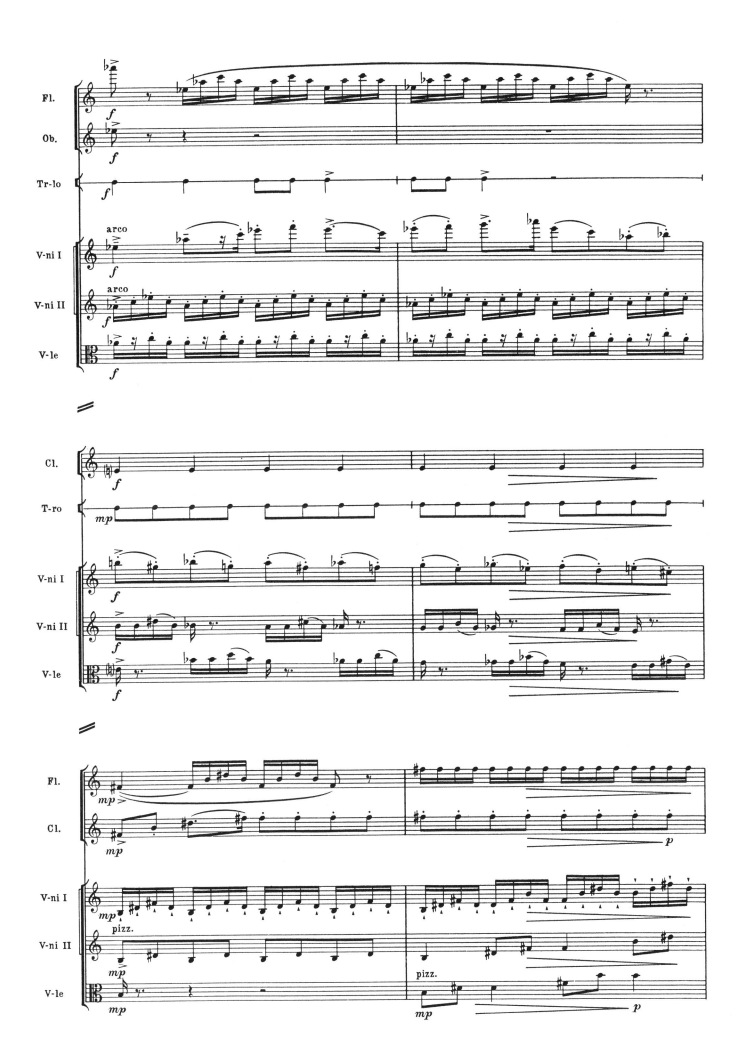

Птичка почти задевала крыльями морду волка, и волк сердито прыгал за ней во все стороны.

The little bird almost touched the wolf's head with its wings while the wolf snapped angrily at it from this side and that.

Ах, как птичка раздражала волка! Как он хотел схватить ее!
Но птичка была ловкая, и волк ничего не мог с ней поделать.

How the little bird did worry the wolf! How the wolf wanted to
catch it! But the little bird was clever, and the wolf simply couldn't
do anything about it.

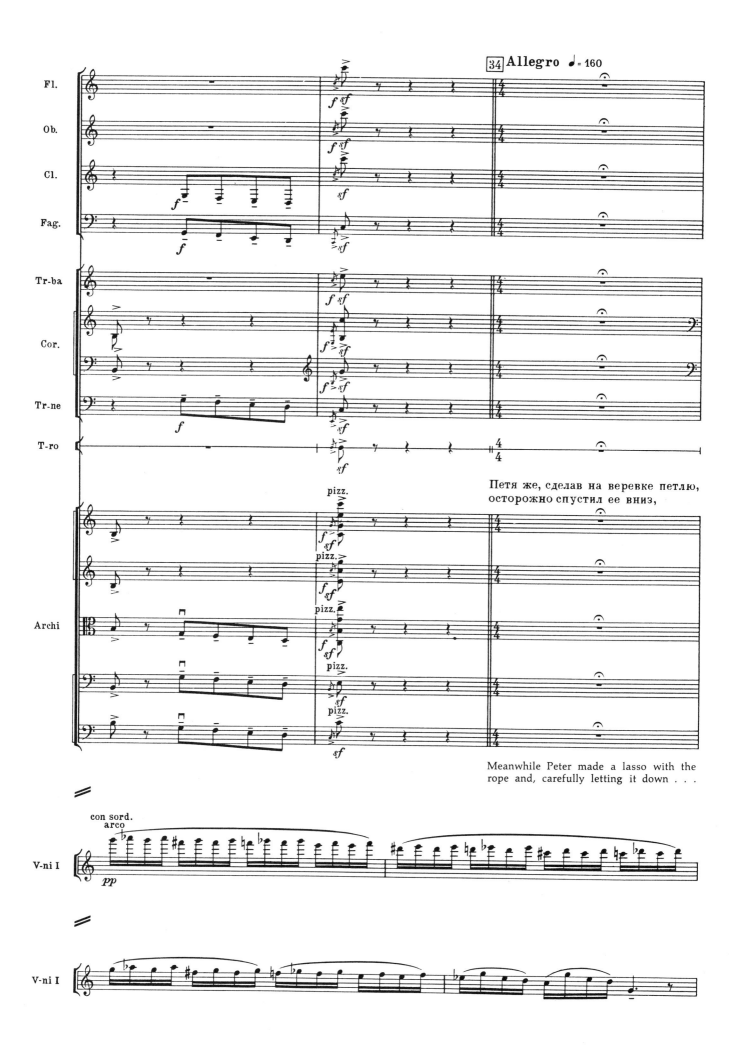

Петя же, сделав на веревке петлю, осторожно спустил ее вниз,

Meanwhile Peter made a lasso with the rope and, carefully letting it down . . .

накинул волку на
хвост и затянул.

. . . slipped it over the
wolf's tail and pulled
with all his might.

Moderato (Meno mosso)

Волк почувствовал, что его поймали, и в бе-
шенстве стал прыгать, стараясь вырваться.

Feeling itself caught, the wolf began to jump
wildly trying to get loose.

Но Петя привязал другой конец веревки к дереву.

But Peter tied the other end of the rope to the tree.

От прыжков волка петля только туже затягивалась на его хвосте.

The wolf's jumping only made the rope around its tail tighter.

В это время...

Just then . . .

из лесу показались охотники.

. . . out of the woods came the hunters.

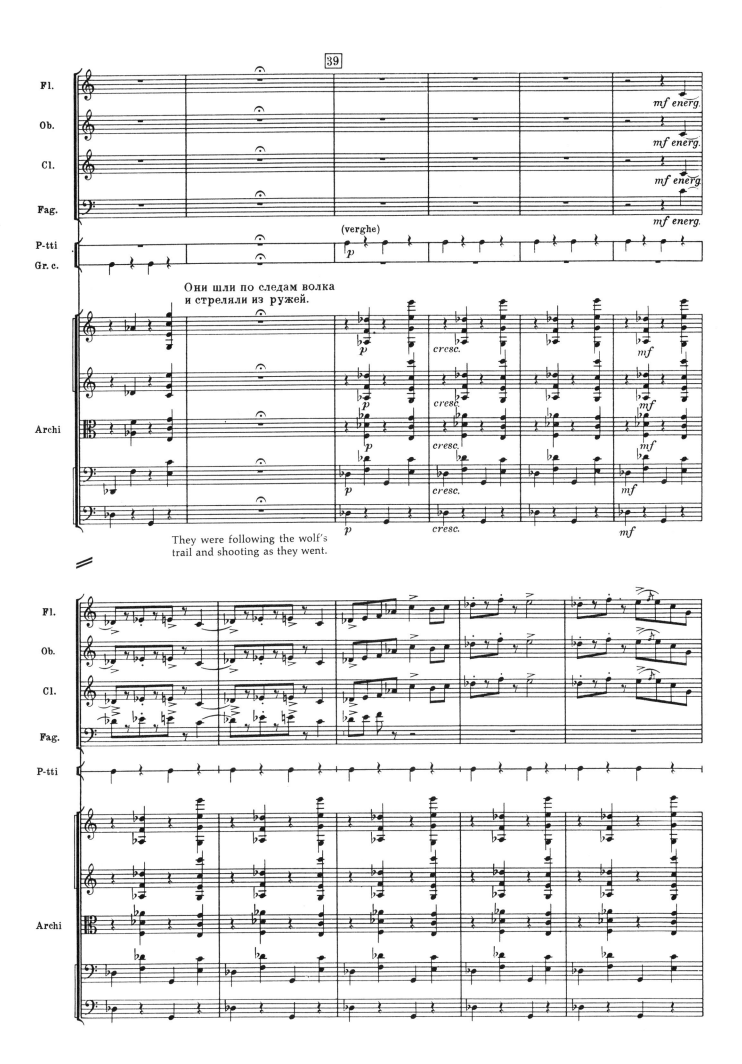

Они шли по следам волка
и стреляли из ружей.

They were following the wolf's
trail and shooting as they went.

Но Петя сказал с дерева: „Не стоит стрелять,
мы с птичкой уже поймали волка! Помогите
отвести его в зоологический сад."

But Peter, sitting in the tree, said: "Don't shoot! The
little bird and I have already caught the wolf. Help
us take it to the zoo."

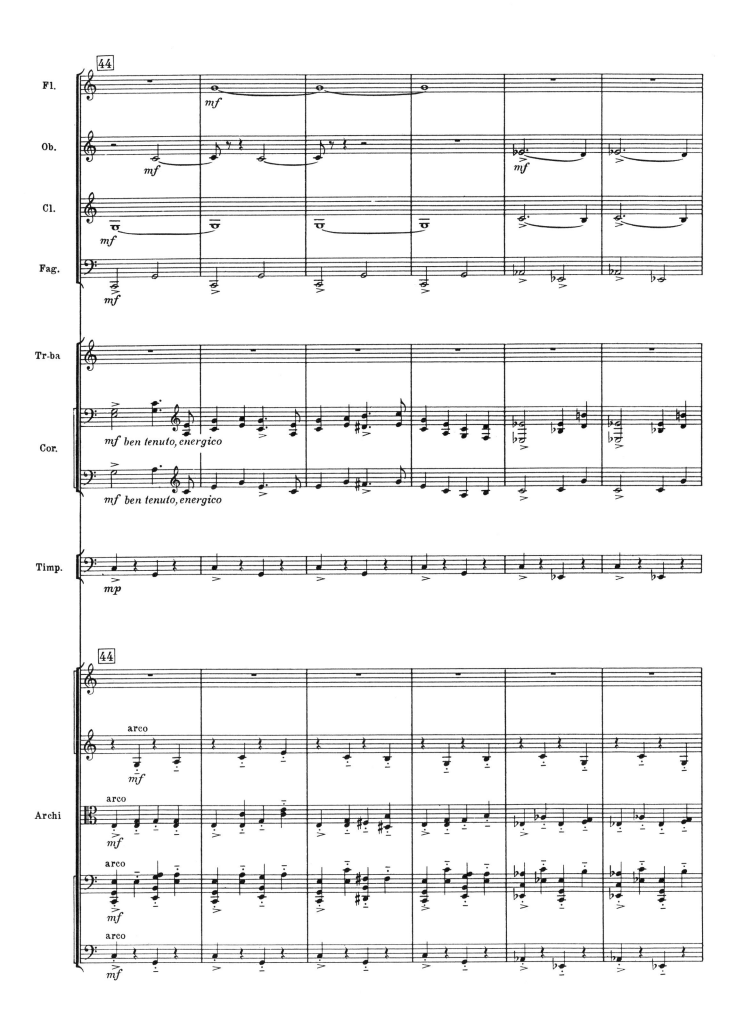

За ним охотники вели волка.

After him the hunters were leading the wolf.

Позади шел дедушка с кошкой. Дедушка недовольно качал головой: „Ну, а если бы Петя не поймал волка? Что тогда?"

And winding up the procession, Grandfather and the cat. Grandfather tossed his head discontentedly: "Well, and if Peter hadn't caught the wolf? What then?"

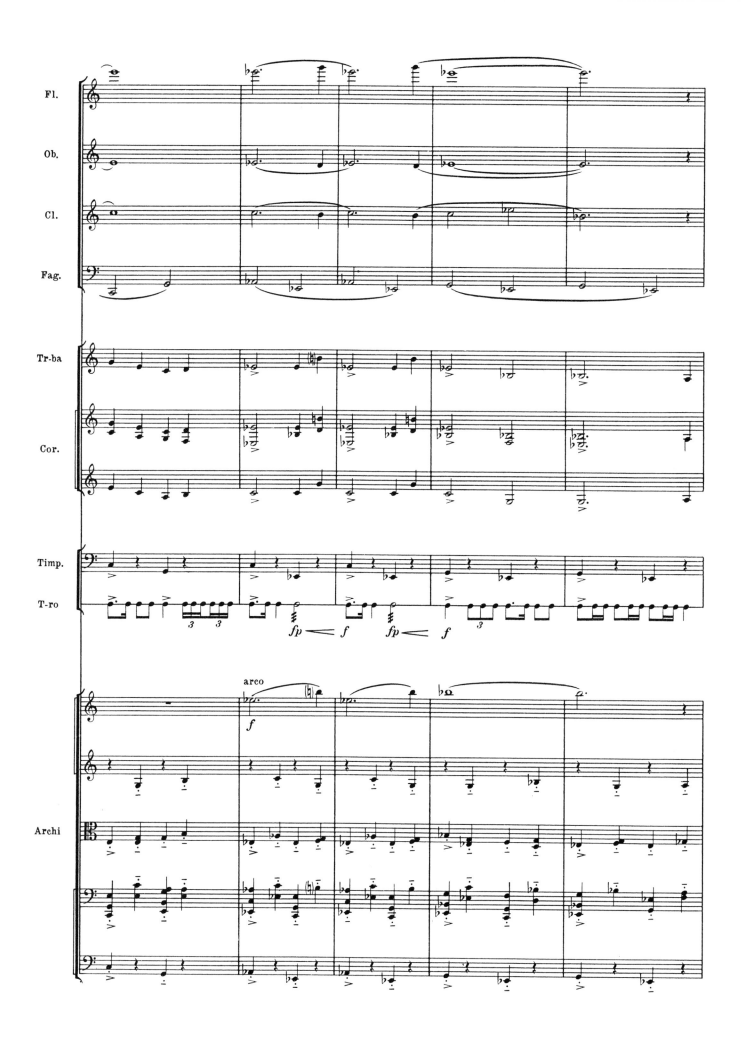

Наверху летела птичка и весело чирикала: „Вот какие
мы с Петей! вот кого мы поймали!“

Above them flew the little bird, chirping merrily: "My, what
fine fellows we are, Peter and I! Look what we have caught!"

А если послушать внимательно, то слышно было, как в животе у волка крякала утка, потому
что волк так торопился, что проглотил ее живьем.

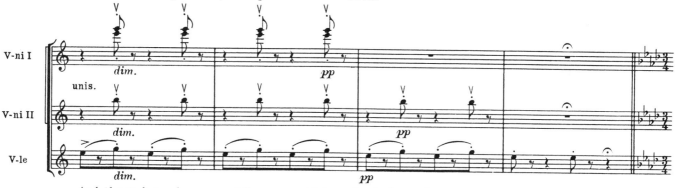

And if you listened very carefully, you could hear the duck quacking inside the wolf's
stomach, because the wolf had been in such a hurry that it had swallowed the duck alive.

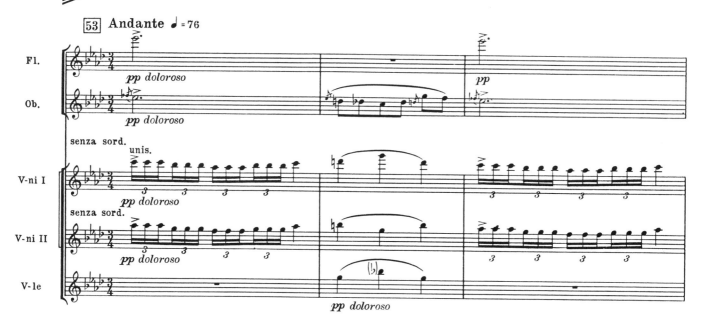

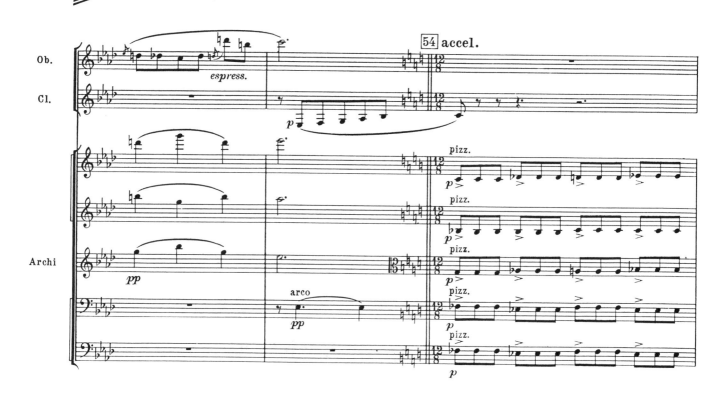

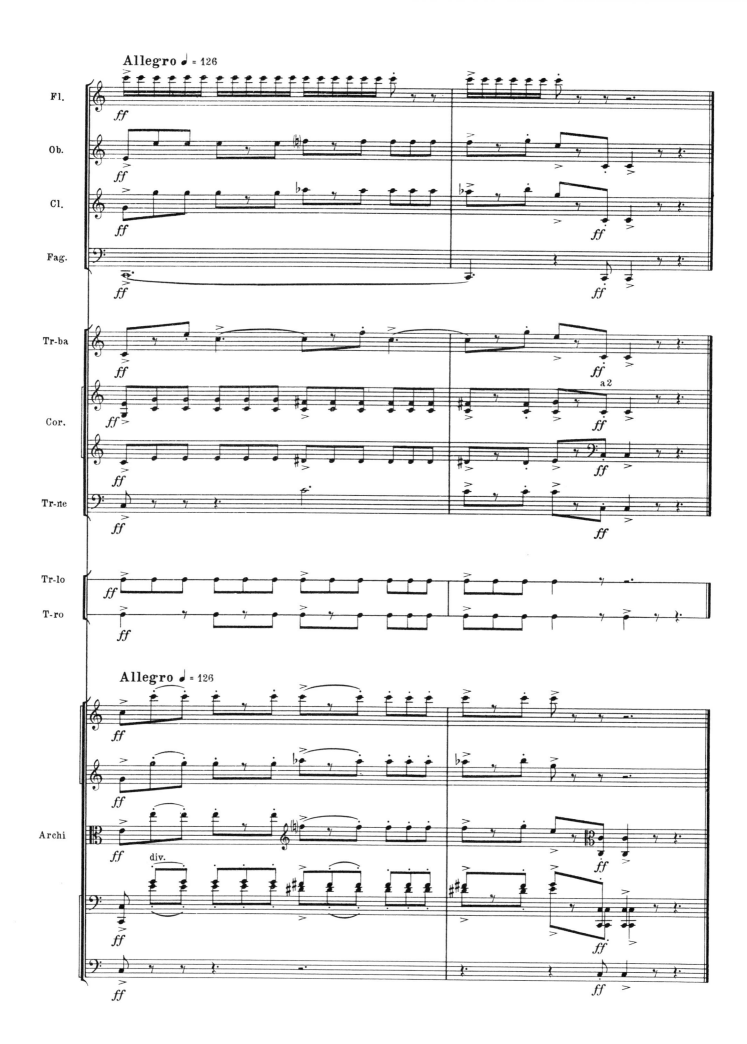

ALEXANDER NEVSKY CANTATA

Op. 78 (1938–1939)

For Mezzo-Soprano, Mixed Chorus and Orchestra
Text by V. Lugovskoy and S. Prokofiev

Instrumentation

Piccolo	Piccolo
2 Flauti	2 Flutes
2 Oboi	2 Oboes
Corno inglese	English Horn
2 Clarinetti	2 Clarinets
Clarinetto Basso	Bass Clarinet
Saxofono	Tenor Saxophone
2 Fagotti	2 Bassoons
Contrafagotto	Double Bassoon
3 Trombe	3 Trumpets
4 Corni	4 Horns
3 Tromboni	3 Trombones
Tuba	Tuba
Timpani	Timpani
Triangolo	Triangle
Tamburo di legno	Wood Block
Tamburino	Tambourine
Tamburo	Snare Drum
Maracas	Maracas
Piatti	Cymbals
Gran cassa	Bass Drum
Tam-tam	Tam-Tam
Campana	Chimes
Campanelli	Orchestra Bells
Silofono	Xylophone
Arpa	Harp
*Violini I	Violins I
Violini II	Violins II
Viole	Violas
Violoncelli	Cellos
Contrabassi	Double Basses

In the score all the instruments are written in C, i.e. as they sound. In the parts, however, the bass clarinet, tenor saxophone and trumpets should be written in B♭, the clarinets in B♭ and A, the English horn and horns in F.

In the score the accidentals for trumpets, horns, timpani, orchestra bells and xylophone are shown in the key signature, but in the parts the accidentals for these instruments should be written next to the notes.

In the fanfares part of the brass instruments use mutes, the other part play without them.

Several fanfares are played offstage, at a distance (in the score: *in distanza*). The return of musicians to their original places is indicated in the score by the word *loco*.

The percussion should be grouped in the following way:

    1. Triangle and Maracas
    2. Tambourine
    3. Snare Drum
    4. Bass Drum
    5. Cymbals and Wood Block

The Tam-Tam is written partly in the 1st part (3rd, 4th and 5th movements) and partly in the 2nd part (7th movement). Therefore, the instrument must be placed between the musicians playing the 1st and 2nd parts. The chime is written, partly in the 3rd part (up to 27) and partly in the 4th part (after 27). Therefore, the instrument must be placed between the musicians playing these parts.

The timpani, xylophone and orchestra bells have separate performers. It is suggested that the harp part be doubled. The chime must be low in tone, otherwise it will not blend with the Tam-Tam.

The maracas is a Cuban instrument used in jazz; it consists of two large nuts filled with dried seeds. The sound of the wood block (*legno*) resembles that of the castanets. If the bass clarinet has no low C (solo at the end of the first movement) this note should be played by the double bassoon.

1. Russia Beneath the Yoke of the Mongols

2. Song About Alexander Nevsky

3. The Crusaders in Pskov

4."Arise, People of Russia"

Под - ни - май - ся, встань, мать род - на - я Русь!

5. The Battle on the Ice

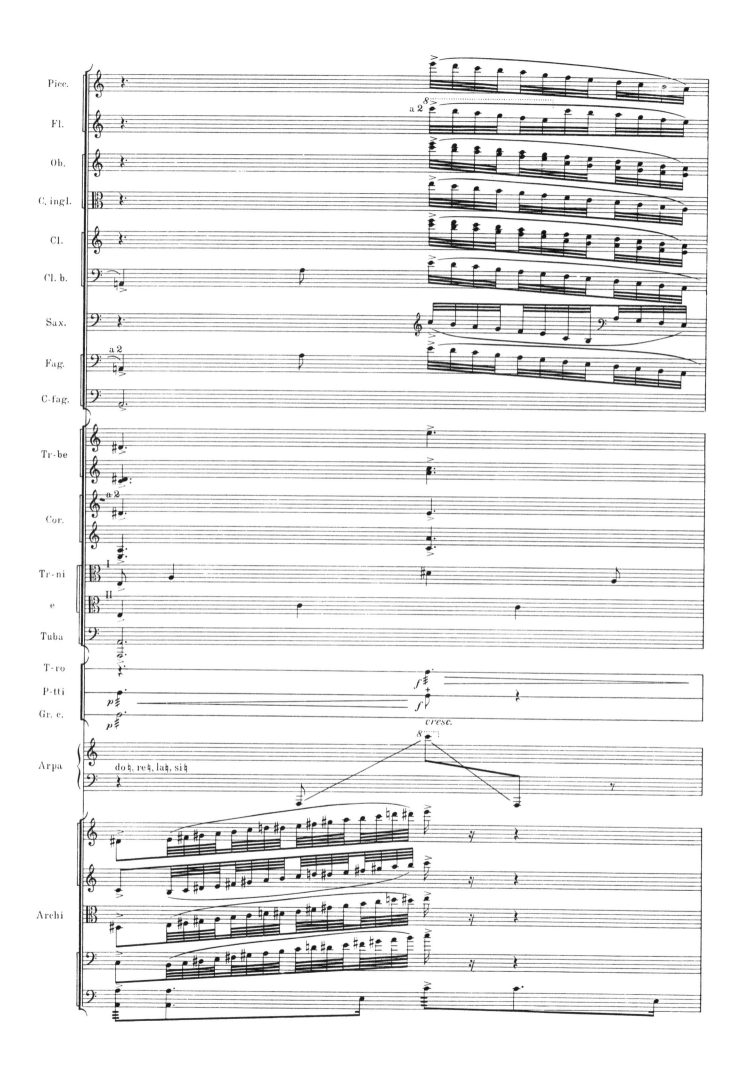

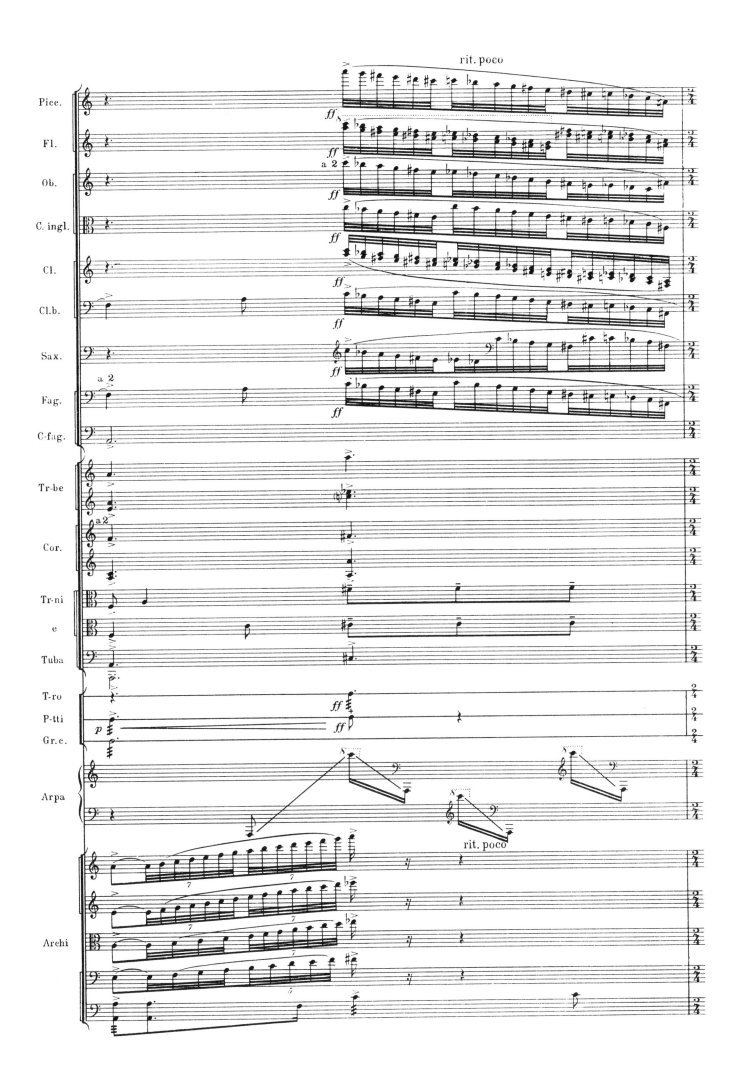

71 Allegretto, quasi doppio movimento

6. The Field of the Dead

7. Alexander's Entry into Pskov

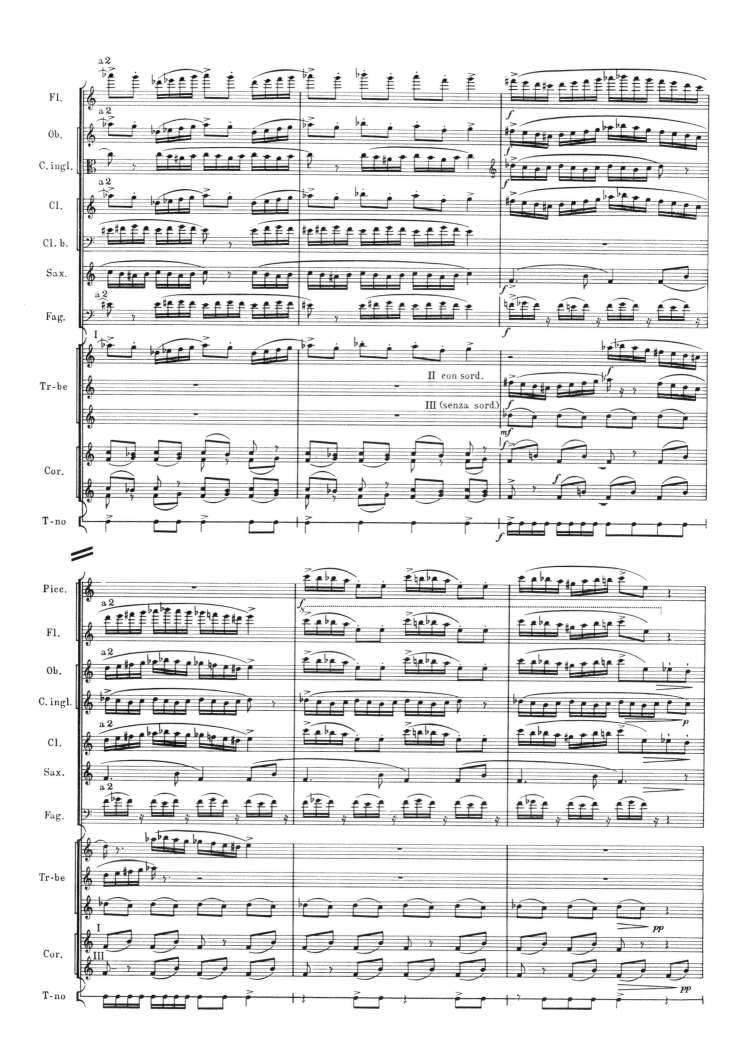

Translations of Vocal Texts

No. 2: Song About Alexander Nevsky

The event was on the Neva River. On the Neva River, on the great water. There we slaughtered the evil army. The evil army, the Swedish forces. Oh, how we fought, how we slashed our way! Oh, we chopped their boats into kindling. We did not spare our golden blood in defense of the great Russian land. Hey! Where the axe passed, there was a street. Where the spear flew, an alley. We mowed down the Swedish enemies like feather-grass on dry ground. We shall not yield up the Russian land. Whoever invades Russia will be killed. Russia has arisen against the foe, arise for battle, glorious Novgorod!

No. 3: The Crusaders in Pskov

A foreigner, I expected my feet to be shod in cymbals.

No. 4: "Arise, People of Russia"

Arise, people of Russia, for the glorious battle, for the deadly battle; arise, free people, to defend our honest land. To the living warriors respect and honor, and to the dead eternal glory. To defend the home of our fathers, to defend Russian territory, arise, people of Russia. Arise, people of Russia, for the glorious battle, for the deadly battle; arise, free people, to defend our honest land. In our native Russia, in great Russia, let no foe exist. Raise yourself up, stand up, our own mother Russia! In our native Russia, in great Russia, let no foe exist. Raise yourself up, stand up, our own mother Russia! Arise, people of Russia, for the glorious battle, for the deadly battle. Arise, free people, to defend our honest land. Let no foe march back and forth through Russia, let no regiments rove across Russia, let them not see the paths to Russia, let them not tread upon the fields of Russia. Arise, people of Russia, for the glorious battle, for the deadly battle; arise, free people, to defend our honest land!

No. 5: The Battle on the Ice

A foreigner, I expected my feet to be shod in cymbals. May the weapons marked with the Cross be victorious! May the enemy perish! A foreigner, I expected my feet to be shod in cymbals.

No. 6: The Field of the Dead

I shall go over the white field, I shall fly over the deadly field. I shall seek the glorious falcons, my bridegrooms, the sturdy young men. One lies hacked by swords, one lies wounded by the arrow. With their crimson blood they have watered the honest soil, the Russian land. Whoever died a good death for Russia, I shall kiss upon his dead eyes, and to that young man who remained alive I shall be a faithful wife, a loving spouse. I shall not marry a handsome man: earthly beauty comes to an end. But I shall wed a brave man. Cry out in answer, bright falcons!

No. 7: Alexander's Entry into Pskov

Russia marched out to the mighty battle. Russia overcame the enemy. On our native soil, let no foe exist. Whoever invades will be killed. Be merry, sing, mother Russia! In our native Russia, let no foe exist. Let no foe see our Russian villages. Whoever invades Russia will be killed. Let no foe see our Russian villages. Whoever invades Russia will be killed. In our native Russia, in great Russia, let no foe exist. In our native Russia, in great Russia, let no foe exist. Be merry, sing, mother of ours! In our native Russia, in great Russia, let no foe exist. Be merry, sing, mother Russia! At the mighty festival all Russia has gathered together. Be merry, Russia, mother of ours!